Understanding Boards of Directors: A Systems Perspective

Other titles in Annals of Corporate Governance

Corporate Governance and Human Resource Management
Geoffrey Wood and Chris Brewster
ISBN: 978-1-68083-188-7

Regulatory Competition in Global Financial Markets
Wolf-Georg Ringe
ISBN: 978-1-68083-146-7

Venture Capital 2.0: From Venturing to Partnering
Joseph A. McCahery and Erik P. M. Vermeulen
ISBN: 978-1-68083-154-2

Fair Value Measurement in Financial Reporting
Leslie Hodder, Patrick Hopkins, and Katherine Schipper
ISBN: 978-1-60198-886-7

The Wolf at the Door: The Impact of Hedge Fund Activism on Corporate Governance
John C. Coffee and Darius Palia
ISBN: 978-1-68083-076-7

Understanding Boards of Directors: A Systems Perspective

Jay W. Lorsch
Harvard University, USA

the essence of knowledge

Boston — Delft

Annals of Corporate Governance

Published, sold and distributed by:
now Publishers Inc.
PO Box 1024
Hanover, MA 02339
United States
Tel. +1-781-985-4510
www.nowpublishers.com
sales@nowpublishers.com

Outside North America:
now Publishers Inc.
PO Box 179
2600 AD Delft
The Netherlands
Tel. +31-6-51115274

The preferred citation for this publication is

J. W. Lorsch. *Understanding Boards of Directors: A Systems Perspective.* Annals of Corporate Governance, vol. 2, no. 1, pp. 1–49, 2017.

ISBN: 978-1-68083-246-4
© 2017 J. W. Lorsch

Editorial Scope

Topics

Annals of Corporate Governancepublishes articles in the following topics:

- Boards of Directors
- Ownership
- National Corporate Governance Mechanisms
- Comparative Corporate Governance Systems
- Self Governance
- Teaching Corporate Governance

Information for Librarians

Annals of Corporate Governance, 2017, Volume 2, 4 issues. ISSN paper version 2381-6724. ISSN online version 2381-6732. Also available as a combined paper and online subscription.

Contents

Understanding Boards of Directors: A Systems Perspective

Jay W. Lorsch

Harvard University, USA; jlorsch@hbs.edu

ABSTRACT

In this essay my goal is to explore why, despite the tireless efforts of talented people, research on corporate governance has been slow and uneven, and where that research should turn to next to be most valuable to practitioners. My belief is that the most fruitful work thus far has recognized that corporate boards are dynamic social systems, has identified all the forces that shape those systems, and has acknowledged that boards should seek to represent a wide variety of *stakeholders*, not just shareholders. The best way for me to establish this argument is to trace the history of research on corporate boards and analyze the trends in that research, including the relative value of the types of data that researchers in this field have used. Ultimately, I identify what I consider to be the best path forward in studying these complex social systems. I have made a deliberate choice to focus primarily on research that reflects firsthand experience with boards rather than on research that utilizes data derived from questionnaires and other secondary sources. Not everyone will agree with my choices, but my hope is that my perspective will nonetheless provide some guidance for people working in this evolving field to understand the true complexity of corporate boards.

Jay W. Lorsch (2017), "Understanding Boards of Directors: A Systems Perspective", Annals of Corporate Governance: Vol. 2, No. 1, pp 1–49. DOI: 10.1561/109.00000006.

1

Introduction

Since the middle of the twentieth century, business and legal scholars have tried to explain why corporate boards of directors function the way they do. These research efforts deserve to be applauded, as it is not easy work to understand what happens behind the closed doors of boardrooms. I have studied corporate governance for 25 years (after previous decades as a teacher and researcher in organizational studies), so I believe that I understand these challenges well.

In this essay, my goal is to explore why, despite the tireless efforts of talented people, research on corporate governance has been slow and uneven, and where that research should turn next to be most valuable to practitioners. My belief is that the most fruitful work thus far has recognized that corporate boards are dynamic social systems, has identified all the forces that shape those systems, and has acknowledged that boards should seek to represent a wide variety of *stakeholders*, not just shareholders. The best way for me to establish this argument is to trace the history of research on corporate boards and analyze the trends in that research, including the relative value of the types of data that researchers in this field have used. Ultimately, I identify what I consider to be the best path forward in studying these complex social systems.

I have made a deliberate choice to focus primarily on research that reflects firsthand experience with boards rather than on research that utilizes data derived from questionnaires and other secondary sources. Not everyone will agree with my choices, but my hope is that my perspective will nonetheless provide some guidance for people working in this evolving field to understand the true complexity of corporate boards.

2

The Roots of Research on Corporate Boards

An understanding of how knowledge-building about large, complex organizations first took shape is crucial to assessing the past research on boards of directors as well as where it should go next. I can identify four stages in the history of this area of study.

2.1 Initial Studies on Organizations

Business research in the initial decades of the twentieth century often focused on understanding worker efficiency and motivation. Perhaps the most notable examples are the time-and-motion studies pioneered by Frederick Taylor and extended by Frank and Lillian Gilbreth. Taylor partnered with factory managers to first break down jobs into their parts, time each part, and then arrange the parts into the most efficient way of working. Taylor's goal was to maximize productivity and improve worker efficiency. The Gilbreths' motion studies had similar aims of explaining how the work was done, how it could be improved, and how to train employees in the best ways to do their work.[1] Obviously, none of this had much relevance to understanding boards.

---

[1] Roser, Christoph, 'The Tale of Taylor and Gilbreth |AllAboutLean.com,' *AllAboutLean* 10 (Nov. 2013), Web. 29 Aug. 2016.

During the same era, work on leadership and organizational structure was first conducted by scholar practitioners like James D. Mooney and Lyndall Urwick, often called the "classical scholars of organization and management."[2] Mooney and Urwick were business executives whose direct experience informed their research.[3] They assumed that workers and executives were rational actors, motivated by economic concerns, who would follow instructions if properly rewarded for doing so. It was not until the 1930s, with the Hawthorne study at the Western Electric factory,[4] and the work of Kurt Lewin[5] and later Chester Barnard,[6] that scholars and practitioners began to consider that leaders and employees were not merely economically rational beings. More systematic research was published on this theme in 1939 when F.J. Roethlisberger and William Dickson wrote *Management and the Worker.*[7] Even then, the research borrowed its methods from the physical sciences and medicine. (Thomas Kuhn's ideas of normal science and research paradigm shifts came much later, as I will discuss.)

2.2   Boards as Rational Legal Entities

While business research was beginning to focus on human activities in organizations, research at this point was still far removed from the boardroom. Although business schools at major universities — most notably the University of Pennsylvania (Wharton) and Harvard University (HBS) — had long since expanded business studies to include

---

[2]Urwick, Lyndall Fownes, 'Organization as a technical problem' (paper read to the Department of Industrial Co-operation of the British Association for the Advancement of Science, September 1933).

[3]Mooney, James D, *The New Capitalism* (New York: Macmillan, 1934).

[4]Western Electric Company Hawthorne Studies Collection, Baker Library, Harvard Business School (accessed December 2015).

[5]Burnes B., 'Kurt Lewin and the Planned Approach to Change: A Re-appraisal,' *Journal of Management Studies* 41:6 (2004).

[6]Scott, Williams G., 'Chester I. Barnard and the Guardians of the Managerial State' (Lawrence, KS: University Press of Kansas, 1992).

[7]Roethlisberger, F. J., W. J. Dickson, Harold A. Wright, and Carl H. Pforzheimer, *Management and the Worker: An Account of a Research Program Conducted by the Western Electric Company, Hawthorne Works, Chicago* (Cambridge, MA: Harvard University Press, 1939).

accounting, finance, manufacturing, marketing, and other topics, the study of boards of directors and corporate governance was still left to university law schools. Scholars assumed that if directors, as rational actors, knew the rules they would follow them. This assumption proved to be misguided, as later history demonstrated. Consider the legal case of *Smith v. Van Gorkom* as discussed by Daniel Fischel.[8] The directors of Delaware-based Trans Union made a decision about an acquisition of the company during the intermission at an opera performance in Chicago. They were later sued by shareholders, who maintained that the directors had violated their legal duty of care by making the decision in this too casual fashion. The Delaware Supreme Court agreed, and the directors were fined and held financially liable, causing consternation among board members nationally and legal authorities in Delaware, who wanted to maintain the state's benign climate for directors. This led to other actions to protect directors in the state from such financial exposure in the future. This case demonstrates that the dynamics that influence boardroom behavior are far more complex than the legal rationality assumption suggests.

As I reflect on these attempts to understand management and later governance, it does seem apt to borrow Kuhn's idea of a paradigm for knowledge-building and scientific activities.[9] In the early years of the study of management, the experience of executives and what seemed to work for them constituted the evidence on how business management and governance should work. There were few or no attempts to study organizations and firms. It was not until the Hawthorne studies of the 1930s that the idea of studying actual human behavior at work gained explicit acceptance as an alternative to relying on only the experience of successful executives.[10] At about the same time, Barnard, who was President of New Jersey Bell, proposed his own set of ideas about leadership

---

[8]Fischel, Daniel, 'The Business Judgment Rule and the Trans Union Case,' 40 *The Business Lawyer* (1985): 1437, 1455.

[9]Kuhn, Thomas S., *The Structure of Scientific Revolutions* (Chicago: University of Chicago, 1970).

[10]Baker Library, *The human relations movement: Harvard Business School and the Hawthorne experiments, 1924–1933* (Cambridge, Mass.: President and Fellows of Harvard College, 2006).

and management.[11] His ideas, along with the others mentioned, created a gradual shift in the paradigm of knowledge-building about business institutions. Most significantly, it led to the recognition that actors in business firms had a broader, more complex set of motivations than just being economically rational.

A paradigm shift of the magnitude of the one that occurred in the field of management and organization could not be a sudden event. Instead, as this shift demonstrates, a change in credible research methods can take years, if not decades. In the case of business research, the paradigm shift began before World War II but is still evolving as the emerging field of behavioral economics demonstrates through writers like Robert Thaler in *Misbehaving.*[12]

2.3 Boards as Complex Decision Makers

The first attempts to examine corporate boards as being more complicated than just legal rational entities were three small studies by HBS faculty between the 1940s and 1971 (Melvin Copeland and Andrew Renwick Towl,[13] and Myles Mace). The nature of these studies is perhaps best reflected in Mace's 1971 book *Directors: Myth and Reality*, which focused on the boards of intermediate-size companies with a majority of outside directors across a range of industries, excluding financial services.[14] Like the company CEOs, these directors were not significant shareholders. Mace collected his data through interviews with these directors, but he revealed neither the number of the interviews nor the methods by which he selected the directors, so I can only assume that he or others at HBS knew them. (In his preface, Mace says he was encouraged to undertake the study by HBS Dean Lawrence Fouraker, who himself served on the board of Citicorp at the time.)

---

[11]Scott, 'Chester I. Barnard and the Guardians of the Managerial State'.

[12]Thaler, Richard H., *Misbehaving: The Making of Behavioral Economics* (New York: W. W. Norton & Company, 2015).

[13]Copeland, Melvin T, and Andrew R. Towl, *The Board of Directors and Business Management* (Boston: Division of Research, Graduate School of Business Administration, Harvard University, 1947).

[14]Mace, Myles L., *Directors: Myth and Reality* (Boston: Division of Research, Graduate School of Business Administration, Harvard University, 1971).

The abstract of Mace's book summarizes his major finding that boards performed three roles. First, boards offer valuable information and routine decision-making assistance to the president (the title CEO was not yet widely used). Second, boards provide discipline to the president and his subordinate management, including the requirement of appearing formally before a board of respected people of high stature. Finally, boards of directors make decisions in crisis situations (*e.g.*, choosing a successor if the president suddenly dies or becomes incapacitated, or replacing the president for very unsatisfactory performance).

Mace contrasted his findings with what he saw as the conventional understanding of the role of boards in the business literature of the time. These included establishing basic objectives, corporate strategy, and broad policies (although presidents usually performed these duties themselves), asking discerning questions (though most presidents did not want directors to do this), and selecting the president (though presidents usually chose their own successors, except in crisis situations). Mace went on to discuss how boards functioned in larger public companies, where shareholders were so dispersed that they had limited power, leaving the choice of direction to the president. He also pointed out that board members were prominent business leaders and professionals who received minimal financial compensation, had limited time, and were primarily motivated to join a board simply as a learning opportunity that conferred high status.[15]

Mace's study was the last of the three initial HBS studies. All three were significant because they were the first attempts by business school faculty to understand what boards did and why. After Mace's study, work that focused on how boards functioned took a hiatus, not just at HBS but everywhere. At the time, these types of studies, drawing on the experience and knowledge of directors, may have been more common at HBS because its alumni and faculty relationships were strong. Thanks to their case writing and research activities, the faculty had a close relationship with companies and their leaders. In addition, it is important to attribute the emphasis of HBS-based studies on the human side of boards largely to many HBS faculty members' interest in

---

[15]Ibid.

the human side of enterprise. Other growing business schools had faculty with a stronger focus on and interest in the discipline of economics as it related to business and, therefore, saw boards solely as agents of shareholders.

2.4   Boards as Servants of the Shareholder

In fact, in the mid-1970s, a new construct explained the role of the board in the context of an economic theory, labeled "agency theory" by Michael Jensen and William Meckling. In their 1976 article "Theory of the Firm, Managerial Theory, Agency Costs and Organization," they explained a new formulation of the relationship among shareholders, managers, and the board — namely that the board's only goal should be to enhance shareholder value.[16] Jensen and Meckling had received their PhDs at the University of Chicago and, at the time their article was published, were on the faculty of the University of Rochester. Later Jensen became a professor at HBS and took these appealing ideas to the MBA classroom, creating a highly popular elective course.

In their article, Jensen and Meckling had pointed to a conflict of interest between shareholders (the principals) and management (the agents engaged to run the firm). Agency theory explained how such conflicts should be resolved when principals and agents had disagreements, different desires, or both. It was the job of the board to resolve these conflicts by ensuring that management acted in the best interest of the shareholders' goal of maximizing value.[17] Their clear, rational theory appealed to directors, to the directors' advisers, accountants, bankers and lawyers, and obviously to many shareholders.

However, agency theory is inconsistent with the law in many U.S. states and parts of Europe. For example, many U.S. states give boards the right and responsibility to make decisions that benefit not only shareholders but also other stakeholders (*e.g.*, employees, surrounding communities) as well as for the long-term survival of the company.

---

[16]Jensen, Michael C., and William H. Meckling, 'Theory of the Firm: Managerial Behavior, Agency Costs and Ownership Structure,' *Journal of Financial Economics* (1976).
[17]Ibid.

And, of course, boards have an obligation to ensure that the company complies with the terms of debt covenants and other contracts. Even in Delaware, where most public companies are incorporated, boards are granted the right, if not the duty, to consider the effect of their actions on parties beyond just the shareholders. Similar provisions also exist in most European countries.

In the U.S. and Europe today, a growing number of business leaders, legal experts and directors themselves argue that agency theory has not only a wrong-headed emphasis, but is also damaging to companies and the economy. They argue that the emphasis on short-term shareholder value is myopic and reduces investment in the longer term (*e.g.*, on R&D, plants, equipment, *etc*). A parallel concern is that an emphasis on shareholder value encourages shareholder activism, which can also compromise long-term corporate investment. Certainly, the view that a board's only goal is to enhance short-term shareholder wealth is simplistic and damaging to any capitalist system that relies on it. Agency theory may have first been articulated 40 years ago, but it still has an effect on how boards function today because many investors and directors accept the idea that a board's only duty is to maximize short-term shareholder value.

3

Demystifying the Dynamics of Corporate Boards

For now, though, I want to return to Harvard Business School, where the next significant attempt to understand the mysteries of corporate board rooms was undertaken. This was the research I conducted with my research associate, Elizabeth MacIver, in 1990.

My motivation for our research developed while I was teaching in a 16-week HBS program for senior executives just below the level of what today we would call the C-suite. As a component of the education for these budding leaders, my faculty colleagues and I wanted to focus part of our curriculum on how boards function, but we had trouble finding material on the topic. We solved our immediate problem by inviting directors we knew personally to discuss their experience in our classes.[18] When I changed assignments at HBS a couple of years later and had more time for research, I decided to undertake a comprehensive study of the topic with MacIver's assistance.

---

[18]Lorsch, Jay W., and Elizabeth MacIver, *Pawns or Potentates: The Reality of America's Corporate Boards* (Boston, MA: Harvard Business School Press, 1989).

3.1　Our Methods

MacIver and I gathered data from directors of major public companies in several ways. First, we sent a questionnaire to 900 directors of S&P 400 companies. We then selected a group of 100 other directors from those same companies for MacIver to interview. Most directors in our sample were from the U.S., but some were from Europe. As the project progressed, we also decided to write four cases about how boards dealt with crisis, leading to interviews with 35 more directors and senior corporate officers.

At first glance, our interests and methods appeared to be similar to those of Mace and his colleagues — to lift the veil of secrecy from corporate boardrooms. However, MacIver and I did not pick boards and individuals to study on the basis of our existing acquaintanceships; instead, we randomly selected our sources, with the intention of getting a representative cross-section of American corporate boards.[19] MacIver and I undertook our study at a time when certain institutional shareholders were criticizing boards, rather severely, for not involving themselves sufficiently in decision-making processes. We wanted to understand whether these criticisms had validity and, if so, how boards could better serve shareholders and society at large.

3.2　Our Findings

We reported our findings in our 1989 book, *Pawns or Potentates: The Reality of America's Corporate Boards.*[20] The title posed the implicit question our study asked: how much real power do corporate boards have over the management of the companies they are intended to oversee? Our findings revealed that corporate boards actually did *not* possess enough power to adequately govern the companies to the extent of what the law required of them.[21] I suppose, in retrospect, this finding should not surprise anyone familiar with corporate boards in the 1990s.

---

[19]Ibid.

[20]Ibid.

[21]Ibid.

More interesting and significant was the manner in which board functioning and the relationship between CEOs and directors created this outcome. As someone who had been educated to the proposition that human groups have systemic properties, I began to sense that boards seemed a lot like a system. In its most simplistic formulation, a system is a set of interrelated factors that together shape the outcome of an entity. All of us on the HBS Organizational Behavior faculty from the mid-twentieth century onward were convinced that business entities (organizational units) had such systemic properties. We were keenly aware of Elton Mayo, F. J. Roethlisberger and William Dickson's participation in the 1920s Hawthorne studies.[22] In addition, there was work by George Homans at Harvard,[23] William White at Cornell,[24] other members of the Harvard Sociology Department, and scholars at London's Tavistock Institute,[25] who argued that such groups were systems. Even before Thomas Kuhn's explanation of the research paradigm,[26] we had realized that the best way to understand work groups, executive teams, boards of directors, and even larger organizational entities, was through the concept of complex social systems.[27]

Although boards needed the power to govern, MacIver and I found that, for several reasons, they lacked that power in relation to company managers. More important, directors depended heavily on the CEO to fulfill their duties as governors. For example the CEO, who was usually also a board chair in the U.S., set the agendas for board meetings, oversaw the information received by directors, and moderated discussions from the head of the boardroom table — all of which greatly affected decision making. Furthermore, the CEO had intimate knowledge of most company operations and, therefore, of the matters being discussed.[28]

---

[22] Supra 7.

[23] For example, Homans, George C., *The Human Group* (New York: Harcourt, Brace, 1950).

[24] For example, Whyte, William F., *Street Corner Society: The Social Structure of an Italian Slum* (Chicago, Ill: University of Chicago Press, 1955).

[25] For example, Rice, A.K., *Productivity and Social Organization: The Ahmedabad Experiment* (Tavistock Publications Limited, 1958).

[26] Supra 9.

[27] Supra 10.

[28] Supra 18.

We also found that the CEOs and directors had unwittingly collaborated to create a system that enhanced the CEO's power over discussions and decisions. In essence, a set of norms about how CEOs and directors should behave enhanced the power of CEOs relative to that of directors. For example, directors were expected to remain uncritical toward the CEO in open boardroom discussions and to refrain from discussing company issues with one another without the CEO present. Therefore, a director might anticipate a crisis months or even years in advance but feel he or she could not, or *should* not, discuss it with other board members.[29] These norms combined to undermine the ability of directors to exercise their power independent of the CEO.

Directors also held widely varying views about their purpose. Some of the board members we interviewed believed they should focus solely on shareholder value, whereas others argued that their goal should be the company's long-term health. A third group on many boards, whom we called "rationalizers," saw the potential conflict between focusing only on shareholder value versus on long-term health and asserted that what was good for the company was also good for shareholders. The fact that such disagreement existed tacitly in many, if not all, boardrooms diminished board power and further increased board dependence on the CEO's leadership.[15] It is worthwhile to note that, in hindsight, all of this was quite inconsistent with the premises of agency theory.

Finally, my work with MacIver revealed important facts about how boards dealt with crises. First, as Mace had found earlier, dealing with a crisis was an important duty of a director.[30] Crises varied from those involving the CEO's behavior and performance to those stemming from product failures, environmental issues, and many other reasons. We also learned that these problems can build up over the course of months or years, or they may appear suddenly and dramatically. Either way, resolving them becomes the board's job and has the potential to take a great amount of time and effort, especially when the CEO is part of the problem at hand. It also became clear that the usual norms of boardroom politeness can further inhibit effective crisis management.

---

[29] Ibid.
[30] Supra 14.

In addition, we found that in dealing with a crisis, boards may rely too heavily on experts (*e.g.*, bankers and lawyers), so much so that they completely lose control of the outcome. For example, former U.S. Attorney General Griffin Bell, a director at Martin Marietta, whom we interviewed for *Pawns or Potentates*, admitted that his board had trusted banker expertise so fully that the directors themselves actually knew too little about the worth of the company they oversaw.[31]

One of the criteria that should be used to judge the quality of any research is its impact on practice. In my (admittedly biased) judgment, *Pawns or Potentates* ranks high in that regard. Our findings effected significant improvements in boardroom practices and in how effectively boards govern companies.

3.3 A Modest Proposal to Improve Corporate Governance

While I may have been responsible for the research and writing of *Pawns or Potentates*, I cannot claim sole credit for its impact on practice. My friend Marty Lipton (of Wachtell, Lipton, Rosen and Katz) helped me develop and spread this knowledge and the innovations that followed. We were also joined by many other individuals in the legal, business, and investment communities. In retrospect, I think we chose a very propitious moment to engage in research on such a topic, or maybe we were just lucky.

My involvement with Lipton came about when, in 1992, I was asked to join a Congressional initiative to improve the competitiveness of U.S. companies. I attended my first meeting in the late summer of that year in Minneapolis, where I met Lipton and others. I remember the date clearly because when the discussion turned to problems of income distribution in the United States and the change that was needed, I commented that the seriousness of the issue was demonstrated by the fact that Clinton and Gore were on their way to Minnesota to campaign around this theme. Most people in the room ignored my comment. In any event, the next committee meeting was in Washington, DC, several months later. At both meetings, I had the opportunity to discuss the

---

[31]Supra 18.

findings of *Pawns or Potentates* with Marty Lipton. At the conclusion of the Washington meeting, he suggested we share a taxi to Regan Airport. As I recall, about half of the ride was spent with Marty on his cell phone. However, during the other half, he and I agreed to write a piece about how boardroom practices could be reformed to enhance the influence of directors in boardroom discussions and decisions. This article appeared in the November 1992 issue of "The Business Lawyer," titled "A Modest Proposal for Improved Corporate Governance."[32]

The changes to board organization and practices that Lipton and I proposed in that article now read like a summary of improvements that have since occurred in North America, Europe, and Australia. Our ideas were initially supported by associations such as the Council of Institutional Investors. However, Top Management groups resisted at first, but entities such as the Business Roundtable, an organization of major company CEOs, soon became supporters. Figure 3.1 is our list of proposals from 1992:

3.4   Intensified Interest in Board Research

Several years later, instances of corporate malfeasance heightened interest in our research on board dynamics. Some examples may help illustrate how dysfunctional boards of directors were tied to serious corporate failings.

Enron, once considered a model of innovation and shareholder profitability, was thrust into the spotlight when it declared bankruptcy in 2001. The subsequent Congressional investigation revealed that significant negligence by the board of directors had been central to Enron's downfall.[33] The Congressional report detailed the numerous ways that Enron's board of directors had failed to adequately shield shareholders from the risky activities undertaken by Enron's top management. Although many of the actions that ultimately destroyed Enron were

---

[32]Lipton, Martin, and Jay W. Lorsch, 'A Modest Proposal for Improved Corporate Governance,' *The Business Lawyer* 48.1 (1992): 59-77.

[33]"The Role of the Board of Directors in Enron's Collapse," United States Congressional Committee on Government Affairs, Subcommittee on Investigations. July 8, 2002.

Smaller boards

- Rationale: Directors know each other better; smaller size faciliates boardroom discussion.

Bi-monthly board meetings of at least one full day

- Rationale: To provide adequate time for the board to do its work.

Selecting a lead director

- Rationale: Given the fact that the Chairman and CEO positions were combined at most U.S. companies, directors would have independent leadership.

Improved information

- Rationale: Information about key performance indicators (that can be understood) supports the board's ability to make decisions.

Corporate and CEO evaluation

- Rationale: The key is an explicit evaluation of the CEO's performance and the performance of the corporation resulting from his leadership. Such an evaluation clearly indicates that the board, not the CEO, is in charge.

Board evaluation

- Rationale: The board will consider explicitly how well is it performing and what changes it can make to enhance its performance.

Meetings with shareholders

- Rationale: Informal meetings with shareholders enable the board to understand any concern or ideas that come from significant shareholders.

Figure 3.1: List of proposals.

Source: Lipton, Martin, and Lorsch Jay W. "A Modest Proposal for Improved Corporate Governance." *The Business Lawyer* 48.1 (1992): 59–77.

enacted by management, including high-risk accounting methods and undisclosed off-the-books partnerships, the board was blamed for allowing such activity to continue unchecked. In addition, the board was criticized for its approval of excessive executive compensation schemes and the fact that some directors' had inappropriately close financial ties to the company.[34] In sum, Enron's board of directors had failed

---

[34]Ibid.

to fulfill its legally required duty to maintain a basic level of oversight, and ultimately contributed to the company's collapse.

The WorldCom board of directors faced similar criticism in the wake of that company's growing debt and ultimate declaration of bankruptcy. In this case, the board seemed to exercise almost no supervision or influence over its company.[35] Large mergers were approved with almost no information, and many actions claiming board approval had actually never been considered by directors. In March 2000, the board of directors allowed WorldCom's CEO and CFO to borrow unlimited funds without board approval. Ensuing investigations found a general apathy toward WorldCom's operations: Many board members were grossly uninformed about the financial processes or the company's culture, and some directors worked as little as three to five hours a year. WorldCom became an example of the dire consequences of a poorly informed and negligent board of directors.

These and other similar events heightened shareholder and public interest in strengthening board members' control over the activities within their companies. There is no question that the increased interest in the research in *Pawns or Potentates* and the article with Lipton was a direct result of the growing public concern about corporate board dysfunction. As a result of the corporate scandals at the turn of the century, the listing requirements of both the NYSE and NASDAQ were modified to include many of our findings.

3.5   International Work on Corporate Boards

While these ideas were disseminated and gradually accepted in the United States, change was also happening in the United Kingdom. The British proposals were not as much the result of academic research, although they may have been informed by it, as of the work of a committee. That committee, established by the Bank of England and chaired by Sir Adrian Cadbury, comprised experienced company leaders, directors, and financial professionals. It proposed changes that the members'

---

[35] Norris, Floyd, 'Ebbers and Passive Directors Blamed for WorldCom Woes,' *The New York Times* (June 10, 2003).

collective experience suggested would improve company oversight by boards of directors.[36] As in the U.S. proposals, the emphasis was on having a board leader who was *not* the CEO (in this instance, a chairman) in addition to independent directors who focused on strategy, company performance, resource allocation, and standards of conduct. Not surprisingly, the British report also focused on issues unique to U.K. boards, such as the role of management directors and the distinction between them and non-management directors.[37]

In subsequent years, two other similar committees in the U.K. provided additional recommendations. In 1995, the Greenbury Report emphasized that executive compensation should be sufficient to attract, retain, and motivate managers, but it also noted that companies should avoid paying more than was necessary.[38] A significant purpose of such compensation was to link executive pay to performance. In 2003, the Higgs Report, formally named "The Review of the Role and Effectiveness of Non-Executive Directors," also through a committee, focused strongly on a non-compulsory approach to board improvement.[39] In other words, boards could deviate from the requirements of such codes if they explained publically the reasons for their deviation. Additional reports with similar messages came in 2009 and 2011. All of these efforts seemed to share the U.S. goal: giving boards the ability (including information and power) to more effectively govern their companies.

In the United States, these changes soon gained the status of mandatory listing requirements by the NYSE and NASDAQ and influenced the Sarbanes-Oxley and Dodd-Frank Federal laws. All of these initiatives, while arguably advancing the cause of superior corporate governance, raise a fundamental question: How important is systematic academic research for improving social and economic institutions like boards? The answer, for me, is that such change can come from different sources

---

[36]Cadbury, Adrian, *Report of the Committee on the Financial Aspects of Corporate Governance* (London: Gee, 1992).

[37]Ibid.

[38]Greenbury, Richard, *The Greenbury Report: Information from the Senior Executive Compensation Group* (London: William M. Mercer, 1995).

[39]Higgs, Derek, *Review of the Role and Effectiveness of Non-Executive Directors* (London: DTI, 2003).

depending on a country's culture and legal infrastructure. Systematic research like that in *Pawns or Potentates* has its role, as do commissions and study groups like those in the U.K. and other countries. What matters most is support for the changes from the broader business, legal, and financial community.

My own interest in the international work leading to board reform was heightened by Jonathan Charkham, who had been an adviser to the governor of the Bank of England and a member of the Cadbury Committee. In 1995, he published a comparative study of the corporate governance systems in France, Germany, Japan, the United Kingdom, and the United States.[40]

3.6   Jonathan Charkham

Unlike the research I have described so far, which focused on how boards functioned internally, Charkham examined how corporate governance was affected by the particularities of the national economic and political systems in which companies operated in these countries. For example, he explored the interconnected nature of German and Japanese companies in each of those countries and the important role of banks in those two nations; the codetermination system in Germany; the limited role of Japanese boards; the unique choice of a one- or two-tiered board system in France; and in the U.S. and U.K., the advocative nature of the board systems, the importance of the CEO, the role of takeovers, and the present and future importance of shareholders. In short, he focused on the broad characteristics of these five systems and how they differed from one another. The takeaway message: boards in different nations may seem similar but can actually vary substantially according to the larger systems in which they operate.

In the same time period as Charkham's book, there were a number of interesting studies on board practices published in the U.K. For example, there was an interview-based study by J. Roberts, T. McNulty, and P. Stiles published in 2005 in the *British Journal of Management*

---

[40]Charkham, Jonathan, *Keeping Good Company: A Study of Corporate Governance in Five Countries* (Oxford: Oxford University Press, 1995).

titled, "Beyond Agency Conceptions of the Work of the Non-Executive Director: Creating Accountability in the Boardroom."[41] This study examined board effectiveness by looking at the work and relationship of non-executive directors. It was based on in-depth interviews with 40 company directors and was commissioned for the Higgs Review. A significant aspect of the article is the observation that research on corporate governance lacks understanding of the behavioral processes and the effects of board of directors. A 1999 study by T. McNulty and A. Pettigrew in *Organization Studies*, titled "Strategists on Boards" examines the contribution to strategy of corporate directors in large companies.[42] The paper askes how, if at all, part-time board members influence strategy in U.K. companies. The data was gathered from interviews with 108 directors and the paper suggests that such directors do not just ratify decisions, they in fact influence the process of strategic choice and control by shaping the ideas and methodologies from which strategic ideas develop.

---

[41] Roberts, J., T. McNulty, and P. Stiles, 'Beyond Agency Conceptions of the Work of the Non-Executive Director: Creating Accountability in the Boardroom,' *British Journal of Management* 16(s1) (2005): S5-S26. doi:10.1111/j.1467-8551.2005.00444.x

[42] McNulty, T., and A. Pettigrew, 'Strategists on the Board,' *Organization Studies* 20(1) (1999): 47-74.

4

The Move Towards Scientific Rigor

In the decades before important early direct research on the social dynamics of corporate boards was being conducted, an influential parallel trend was also taking shape. Beginning in the 1960s, business school curricula and research practices came under scrutiny and pressure from several sources, most notably the Carnegie and Ford foundations and then Harvard University president Derek Bok in the U.S.. In short, these critics sought more rigor in teaching and research at business schools. That, to their minds, meant hiring business school faculty with graduate degrees in the social science disciplines so that they might adopt the research paradigms of those disciplines — specifically, more-systematic data collection and analysis. This shift stemmed from the criticism among academics that business research was too anecdotal, case-based, and lacking in quantitative analysis, compared with research in fields such as economics.[43]

In 1979, Derek Bok wrote a Harvard "President's Report," in which he argued that having more HBS business faculty trained in the social sciences would strengthen the quality of research at the school by

---

[43]Bok, Derek, *Higher Education in America.* (Princeton University Press, 2013).

combining field-based and theoretical methods.[44] Such calls for change began to influence the research paradigm in the field of management and governance within business schools. More and more articles began to appear in peer-reviewed journals. This shift paralleled the rapid growth of computers as research tools. These trends combined to the effect that most research on boards being conducted by young academics relied on quantitative analytic tools. In a sense, this made it easier for these young researchers to get publicly available quantitative data. But it also meant that the sources of their research could not — and did not — capture the systemic nature of boards.

I had two reactions to this trend. First, I felt that the survey methods we had used in *Pawns or Potentates* were consistent with more systematic research. Second, I was dubious that the call for more sophisticated quantitative analysis would be able to shed light on the complexities of boards inner functioning. Although I had not yet explicitly articulated this point of view in a published article, I thought of boards (or any organization or small group) as a social system and did not see how large-scale, data-heavy research could help us better explain boards' social dynamics. My skepticism, however, was not shared by other researchers in the field. These types of studies exploded, which, as I have just suggested, was likely a result of their appeal to young researchers who could not gain direct access to boards of directors.[45]

4.1   The Research of Westphal and Zajac

In my opinion, the best example of this type of research is the collaborative work of two American organizational scholars, James Westphal and Edward Zajac. Starting in 1988, they began to publish their research on corporate boards in scholarly journals — 17 articles in all, coauthored and with other collaborators. (See Appendix exhibit 1 for examples.) They used publicly available data about corporate boards

---

[44]Bok, Derek, *President's Report*. (Cambridge, MA: Harvard University Press, 1979).

[45]Fiss, P., and E.J. Zajac, 'The Diffusion of Ideas Over Contested Terrain: The (Non)adoption of a Shareholder Value Orientation Among German Firms,' *Administrative Science Quarterly* (2004).

and their members as their sources, as well as surveys conducted by their research teams. The work was informed by concepts and prior research in social psychology and sociology, as well as earlier studies of corporate boards.[46]

This impressive body of work captured my attention for its methodology and its connection with research in the social sciences. Yet, in my view, it lacked a cohesive perspective on the totality of the forces that shape boardroom behavior and on the changes in relationships within boards and, especially, between directors and managers in the U.S. and Europe during the 1990s.

In short, Westphal and Zajac often arrived at what I saw as too simplistic an explanation of cause and effect. For example, in a 1996 *Administrative Science Quarterly* article, they proposed that powerful top managers seek to maintain their control over the CEO by selecting and retaining board members who have experience on other passive boards. They also argued that powerful boards sought to maintain their control by favoring directors who had a reputation for more-active oversight of management.[27] This research was based on historical data and, therefore, overlooked the important trend toward increasing power among directors that was taking place in real-world boardrooms of the time.

Similarly, in their 1988 article "The Dynamics of CEO–Board Relationships," Zajac and Kimberly argued that the relationship between the CEO and the board reflects both a significant gap in the research literature and a particularly fertile domain for research about corporate performance.[47] On this point they were prescient. Much of the data in *Pawns or Potentates* focused on the relationship between CEOs and directors.

Furthermore, I had a concern that the findings in these articles derive from statistical methods that do not explain causation. Also, the degree to which CEOs or directors actually understand the prior experience or perspectives of new directors is also hard to predict, not

---

[46]Phone conversation with Edward Zajac, 2015.

[47]Zajac, Edward J., and James D. Westphal, 'Director Reputation, CEO-Board Power, and the Dynamics of Board Interlocks,' *Administrative Science Quarterly* 41.3 (1996): 507–29

to mention that new directors and CEOs might respond differently in different board situations. As much as I find their studies impressive, the fact remains that the way board decisions are made, including who is most influential at the boardroom table, can be understood only by observing the meetings in real time or, although less desirable than firsthand observation, by interviewing directors about how they experience what happens in these meetings.

Westphal, Zajac, and their colleagues dutifully followed the protocols of the social science paradigm of data collection and analysis, and the number of their publications reflect the quality of their methods and reporting. Clearly, they have been among the most prolific and significant researchers on corporate boards. And their work is indeed as good as one can expect given the constraints of this type of data collection and the research paradigm of the social sciences today. Nonetheless, it does not provide a comprehensive view of the complex behavior that characterizes boardroom decision-making.

The most important indicator of success for young academics in the social sciences is to publish articles in so-called "A Journals." Zajac, Westphal, and their coauthors were certainly successful in this regard. For example, seven of their articles listed in the Appendix were published in such journals. That success, coupled with growing interest in corporate boards (thanks to the high-profile failures at WorldCom, Enron, and elsewhere), led to an increase in articles about boards in peer-reviewed journals, including *Corporate Governance: An International Review.* In short, there was a confluence between public interest in board dynamics and a proliferation of academic publishing driven by social science methodology.

Given my ambivalence about the work of Westphal and Zajac, I decided that it was important to seek their own perspective on their body of research. So I approached them directly, and they graciously agreed to talk to me, each separately in 2016.[48] For starters, I learned that both men became interested in corporate boards as PhD students — Zajac at Wharton and Westphal at Kellogg, where Zajac was Westphal's thesis adviser. Zajac called himself "a strategy guy" who became interested in

---

[48]Phone conversation with Edward Zajac and James Westphal, 2016.

boards because they, along with top managers, were heavily involved in strategic decision-making. Before Kellogg, Westphal had worked as an executive compensation consultant and was intrigued by the role of boards in these matters. Feeling it would be difficult, if not impossible, to study boards in action by attending board meetings, they chose to collect data via the best alternative: publicly available sources and surveys of board members. Zajac and Westphal said that they each recognized the limits of these methods but believed they were the only options available. So they followed the social science paradigm in terms of data collection and analysis — and published prolifically.

My interviews with Westphal and Zajac made me even more impressed by the volume, scope and quality of their work. Yet I still was concerned about the work's lack of direct insight into the complex decision-making behavior in boardrooms. The most interesting moments of both interviews came when each of the men identified outright what needed to take place in future research: firsthand observation of boardroom behavior.

Zajac, who currently serves on boards, was particularly articulate on this point. After telling me how much he has learned from observing boards as a director, he went on to emphasize the value of observation in knowledge-building more generally: "Take Einstein on a trolley in Zurich, or Newton getting hit by an apple falling off a tree," he said. "It is the observation of the phenomenon that is important. Some people believe that knowledge and understanding come from a guy in a lab or an office staring at the wall. No, new ideas come from observation."[49] This is a very astute point, but the problem is that observation by non-directors is not allowed in boardrooms, which leads me to the next phase of my argument.

---

[49]Phone conversation with Edward Zajac, 2015.

5

The Constraints on Gathering Evidence

The only people who can attend board meetings are board members, senior managers invited by the board, and professional advisers. Unfortunately, that leaves the people who conduct research about boards with the dilemma of gathering evidence indirectly.

5.1 The Limitations of Quantifiable Data

Thus, the basic problem has been that the only people who could attend board meetings were board members, as well as invited members of senior management and professional advisers. For legal and competitive reasons, attendance of board meetings by anyone else was and still is restricted. Such limitations are certainly reasonable from a company perspective; however, the consequences for those trying to understand boards is that you need to rely on indirect methods, such as those that Westphal, Zajac, and their colleagues employed, to grasp how boards function.

In contrast, the early HBS researchers interviewed board members to gather accounts of the actual behavior in the boardroom. The specific interview data and highly detailed survey responses we used to inform

Pawns or Potentates yielded greater nuance than one can extract from large datasets. For example, MacIver and I were able to analyze the questions directors asked at board meetings, including their articulated reasons for accepting and refusing board membership, their views on the personal benefits of board service, long-term versus short-term considerations in decision making, information they received in advance of meetings, specific agenda items, the details of directors' contributions and influence at meetings (and the constraints on that influence), and the degree and sources of the CEO's power.

It would be a great overstatement to say that we arrived at an overarching explanatory theory of board dynamics, but we did gain crucial insight into interdependent relationships, even though they were not quantifiable. Such a conceptual scheme was akin to what Roethlisberger called a "walking stick" to guide one's understanding of group dynamics.[50]

5.2   Data That Reflect the Complexity of a Social System

Our book *Pawns or Potentates* represented an important step in gathering nuanced, qualitative data, but I freely admit that its stated mission was not to use that information to explain how boards functioned, but more simply to show that boards did not behave as legal requirements expected them to do. My understanding of the bigger picture crystallized in 1999, when I met Colin Carter.

Carter, an HBS alumnus who was then a senior vice president of the Boston Consulting Group in Melbourne, Australia, was introduced to me by my friend and Carter's colleague Mark Blaxill. Carter had been advising boards of directors in Asia and the Pacific Rim for 25 years. Blaxill suggested that Carter and I collaborate on a book about why boards still found it difficult to be effective on both sides of the Pacific, and we set out to do just that.

Carter and I recognized that boards' use of general best practices was not adequate for solving all of the issues confronted by particular

---

[50]Roethlisberger, F.J., *The Elusive Phenomena* (Cambridge, MA: Harvard University Press. 1977).

boards. We started with the hypothesis that each board faced issues that were specific to its company; the board's relationship with management at that company; and the board's size, legal duties, director experience, and structure. When crises erupted at Enron, Tyco, WorldCom, and less well-known examples globally, we focused more on how and why such scandals occurred even when boards tried to be diligent.

Data-gathering for our book, ultimately titled *Back to the Drawing Board*,[51] was obviously central to the project. In addition to relying on our experience and that of our colleagues, we developed a detailed questionnaire for the CEOs of BCG's clients in North America, Europe, and the Asia/Pacific region (137 companies in all). We chose to survey CEOs because we had earlier obtained data from directors themselves in *Pawns or Potentates*.

Some of our colleagues warned that CEOs might paint too rosy a picture of their boards in order to discourage board reforms that would further limit CEO power. However, we found something more striking: CEOs often believed that directors were uninformed about company matters and were quite open in expressing that point of view. More important, our qualitative data helped us identify the factors that affected how boards defined and executed their governance responsibilities. At one extreme, some boards behaved like watchdogs by sitting back, observing management decisions, and taking an active role only when they saw danger. At the opposite extreme, other boards chose to behave like a pilot actively steering a vessel into the harbor. Each board fell somewhere on this spectrum depending on its particular capabilities, circumstances, and management structure and team.[52]

Using this nuanced qualitative data, Carter and I concluded that each board was subject to unique circumstances that influenced how the board behaved. In short, boards adopted a pattern of behavior in response to the demands and resources (knowledge, time, information, and group dynamics) of their system. Did they decide on their behavioral

---

[51]Lorsch, Jay W., and Colin Carter, *Back to the Drawing Board: Designing Corporate Boards for a Complex World* (Boston, MA: Harvard Business School Press, 2003).

[52]Ibid.

patterns consciously? Most likely not. But we did conclude that boards should design their activities to fulfill a role appropriate to their company with its own unique circumstances and challenges.[53]

The question we must now consider is whether a scientific approach driven by statistics and quantitative analysis — like that of Westphal, Zajac, their colleagues, and many others — is the preferable method for explaining how and why boards function as they do. Or is it more useful to analyze boards as social systems by using narrative, qualitative, largely non-numerical data? Given my background and research experience, I clearly favor the latter. But the optimal way to obtain such qualitative data is obviously to get inside boardrooms to attend actual board meetings, which, as I've noted, is very difficult, if not impossible, to do. All boards are required to keep minutes of their meetings, but these documents are typically recorded by company lawyers who are well-trained in how to create minutes that meet the legal requirements but do not provide sufficient detail to elucidate the dynamics of board discussions. That brings me to two studies that have managed to use direct observation of boards as their data source.

5.3   Directly Observed Data

Before I discuss these two studies, I should acknowledge that there are, of course, published accounts of boardroom discussions written by people who have served on boards. I admire the intentions and efforts of those writers, but I know from serving on boards myself that it is very difficult to report objectively on boardroom deliberations when you are also a participant. These accounts have their own value, but they are not a substitute for work done by dispassionate observers.

The most ambitious attempt that I am aware of to observe boards in action is aptly titled *Inside the Boardroom*.[54] The authors were Richard Leblanc (who started the research for his doctoral dissertation at York University in Canada) and his dissertation adviser James

---

[53]Supra 51.

[54]Leblanc, Richard, and James M. Gillies, *Inside the Boardroom: How Boards Really Work and the Coming Revolution in Corporate Governance* (Mississauga, Ont: J. Wiley & Sons Canada, 2005).

Gillies, who had served on the boards of 30 companies. Their research involved observing the boards and board committees of 21 companies and interviewing almost 2,000 directors. In the book, the authors explain in detail the steps they took to gain access to board meetings, including two appendices on their methodology for negotiating the terms of access to meetings and to individual directors. Leblanc and Gillies deserve great credit for achieving the kind of access that allowed them to develop such a rich evidence base.

Their book begins with a nod to changing board practices, some of which I have described above in my list of modest proposals. Leblanc and Gillies point specifically to smaller boards, more-effective chairmen, clearer board processes, and better delineation of board tasks. Most significantly, they emphasize the importance of the selection of quality directors. Leblanc and Gillies understood that boardroom behavior is a function of a system of forces. They refer to boards as "open systems" and recognize that it is difficult to establish a clear causal relationship between boardroom behavior and company financial performance, a similar conclusion to mine and Carter's in *Back to the Drawing Board*. Leblanc and Gillies do conclude, however, that boards constructed according to their model should be more likely than not to accomplish their assigned tasks.

Leblanc and Gillies also argue that, although board decisions are influenced by many factors, the specific competencies and behavioral characteristics of the directors and how the directors interact with one another are the ultimate determinants of effective decision making. They identify three characteristics that determine directors' effectiveness: persuasive versus non-persuasive, consensus-building versus dissenting, and collectivist versus individualistic.[55] They also categorized directors as those who had five positive (functional) behavioral characteristics (see Appendix exhibit 2) and those who had five negative (dysfunctional) behavioral characteristics (see Appendix exhibit 3). They claim that boards with functional directors were more effective than those with dysfunctional directors.[56]

---

[55]Ibid. 163–164.
[56]Ibid.

The lack of detail in the presentation of these data makes it impossible to verify independently the authors' conclusions, but their argument seems reasonable. However, there remains a missing link: how directors' behavioral characteristics mesh with other elements of the boardroom social system. The authors expend enormous effort in identifying and explaining directors' behavioral characteristics, which do matter. However, they give short shrift to the social systems in which these personal characteristics thrive or fail.

Interestingly, the authors devote their final two chapters to a version of the point Carter and I made in *Back to the Drawing Board.*[57] They argue that successful boards must have qualities that fit the issues the company is facing, as well as its strategy. They also state that boards, like the companies they oversee, are dynamic and must adapt to change.[58] My guess is that this important conclusion took a back seat to the more sensationally appealing framework (useful as it is) of behavioral personality types. What Leblanc and Gillies got right was the method of deriving analysis from direct observation. Where they went astray, in my view, was in limiting the major scope of their argument to the personal traits of directors at the expense of analyzing the context of the social system.

I became familiar with this next study of boards by working with Katharina Pick, a PhD student at HBS and in Harvard's sociology department. Her attempt to observe boards in action for her dissertation was more modest in scale than that of Leblanc and Gillies — but it was nonetheless quite successful.

Pick was able to get direct access to the boards of five public mid-cap companies. The deal she negotiated allowed her to observe three board meetings of each board, but only to report on the frequency and patterns of interaction among the participants. She found that, at all 15 board meetings she observed, there was a clear pattern: About 80% of the directors' interactions were with management. Given the common complaint that boards lack sufficient time to accomplish all that is expected of them, the fact that so much time is spent in discussions between directors and managers is disturbing. Indeed, it raises the

---

[57]Supra 51.
[58]Supra 54.

question of how to create more time for discussion among the directors themselves.[59]

Pick's finding highlights the power of observation as a research tool. Her work revealed that the astute human observer is able to discover phenomena that are difficult to capture in any other way. When I reflect on my own time serving on boards (four public company boards and several other private-company boards) and consulting to many others, I observed many board meetings even though I was not studying them as a researcher. This exposure confirmed my sense that boards are social systems. Boards had certain tasks in common (*e.g.*, meeting dates tied to earnings-release dates, reports from the CEO to the board, meetings with management to discuss past results and future plans), but there were always important differences related to the nature of the company and its business issues. On some boards, directors took only a broad view of strategy; on others, they got deeply involved in discussing strategic options. Such differences were tied to each company's circumstances (such as CEO tenure, company size and diversity, and performance). I also became aware that boards, like other social systems, observed their own social norms about how members should participate according to their tenure and experience. They had their own (often tacit) ways of enforcing these informal rules, such as becoming restless when someone talked too much or actually cutting a colleague off mid-sentence.

After a few years of such observations, I had the opportunity to learn firsthand how effective boards responded in an unanticipated crisis. Whether in the context of a dispute with a CEO about his successor, how to respond to an unanticipated takeover bid, or how to deal with management malfeasance, I observed that an important quality of effective boards was having a sufficient number of directors who would step up and work together to resolve the crisis. Often these were not the individuals with formal board positions, but rank-and-file directors who felt the responsibility to step up. And I have always been impressed by how board social systems adjusted to make such changes possible.

---

[59]Lorsch, Jay W., A. Zelleke, and Katharina Pick. 'Unbalanced Boards,' F0102E. *Harvard Business Review* 79(2) (February 2001).

6

Why Board Research Should Focus on Social Systems

The final leg of my journey in discovering that corporate boards must be studied as social systems came from my contact with Rakesh Khurana and the aforementioned Katharina Pick, who together articulated a social system perspective on boards in their 2007 article, titled "The Social Nature of Boards," in the *Brooklyn Law Review.*[60]

Khurana and Pick recognized that most of the prior scholarship on boards focused, incorrectly, on the qualities of individual actors rather than on the ways in which those actors perform dynamically in a social system. They acknowledged that prior research (such as mine with MacIver and that of Westphal and Zajac) had hinted at this fact, but they were much more direct in this assertion. They wrote: "A board is not a simple aggregation of individuals, but is in fact a complex social system and ought to be understood as such."[61] They go on to highlight the power of groups:

> We know from decades of research on groups that they are enormously powerful social environments. Group influences

[60]Khurana, Rakesh and Katharina Pick. 'The Social Nature of Boards,' *Brooklyn Law Review* Vol. 70. (2005).

[61]Ibid.

on individuals as well as factors that emerge purely at the group level and through the group situations in a wider social context shape member behaviors, beliefs, and attitudes. Our argument is that in order to understand the factors that contribute to board culture and board outcome, whether dysfunctional or functional, we must treat boards as complex social systems, and use the group as the basic unit of analysis when we study them. We must understand both the factors that are driven by group dynamics and culture and those that result from environmental influences on the board.[62]

As I reread their words from 2005, about the same time as Carter and I were writing *Back to the Drawing Board,* I cannot help but wonder why he and I were not as explicit as Khurana and Pick. At the time, we all were in frequent discussions about their ideas and my research with Carter. As in many research endeavors, it is hard to know who influenced whom about what.

Nevertheless, in their writings, Khurana and Pick focused much more explicitly on contrasting the social nature of boards as groups with the more individual-focused perspective on boards in prior research. They went on to point out other social dynamics that could vary among boards but were important characteristics of all board social systems. Although most boards are relatively small (9 to 12 members), they often vary in their cohesiveness because most directors are high-status, independent-minded individuals with leadership experience in business.[63] Khurana and Pick also stressed that norms of behavior (informal rules about how directors were supposed to act with one another and with managers) varied considerably, with consequent effects both within and outside of board meetings — a finding we had noted in *Pawns or Potentates.*[64]

Although Carter and I were conceiving of boards as systems in *Back to the Drawing Board,* our explicit focus was not as much on the social

---

[62]Ibid.

[63]Ibid.

[64]Supra 18.

nature of the systems as on the tasks the systems needed to accomplish, the nature of the strategic and performance issues confronting the boards, the challenges and problems the board faced, the knowledge and time the board had to grapple with these issues, and so on. It is in the intersection between how boards function as social groups and how tasks get accomplished through social protocols that research on board dynamics has its richest potential, particularly when opportunities to access boardrooms directly (like that of Leblanc and Gillies and Khurana and Pick) arise.

6.1 Why "Teams" Are an Inadequate Concept for Board Dynamics

Nowadays, many scholars seem to want to incorporate all work on group dynamics under the umbrella of research about teams, and many practitioners imply that it is desirable for all groups to behave as teams. But those propositions can be problematic for corporate boards. Disagreements on a board are not merely hurdles to overcome in order to achieve a common goal. Rather, disagreement is innate to a board's responsibilities. There is often important disagreement and dissent among the various directors and between the board and management. In such a context, a team mindset might even be counterproductive.

Nevertheless, many senior executives (including CEOs) and board members hold on to the idea that the board and top management must collaborate as a team to take action about corporate decisions. However, the board is being asked not only to take joint action with management but also to judge the wisdom of the decisions in which it has participated. Although effective governance requires open dialogue between the board and management and, hopefully, eventual agreement on action, the possibility of disagreement must be left open, by design, if the board is to fulfill its responsibility. That may seem like a complicated proposition — and it is.

Instead, what a board needs are norms of civil conversation and discussion for its internal deliberations and for its interactions with management. But in the end, the ultimate decision maker is the board.

That, after all, is what the law says. Boards and their leaders may not like to force management to accept the board's recommendations, but they have the legal right (and obligation) to do so. This dynamic makes the corporate board social system incompatible with the "team" framework.[65]

---

[65]Edmondson, Amy C. *Teaming: How Organizations Learn, Innovate, and Compete in the Knowledge Economy*, (San Francisco: Jossey-Bass, 2012).

7

A New Paradigm for Board Research

So far in this essay, I have outlined the development of board research in academia and suggested that a data-dependent research approach like that of Westphal and Zajac and most others is incapable of capturing the systemic dynamics of boards. I have provided examples from my own work as well as research conducted by others in which firsthand observation has permitted a deeper analysis of the board as a complex social system. I have also acknowledged the challenges inherent to pursuing research on corporate boards. However, before I can share my advice about how best to overcome these obstacles, I must address the key questions raised in the beginning of this essay. Why do scholars research boards and how does this research affect real practice?

I would argue that research on corporate boards is done by academics for three primary reasons. First, academics like to study *power*. Boards are intrinsically powerful institutions, made up of powerful people making powerful decisions about powerful corporations. Scholars have long been attracted to studying and understanding such phenomena, so it comes as no surprise that those studying business institutions today are drawn to corporate boards.

The second reason for the popularity of researching boards can be found in the short-term incentive system for young budding academics.

Because young academics are faced with minimal time and limited access to information, boards — and especially board failures — are fertile ground for publication-worthy research. As I have mentioned, junior academics are under extreme pressure to publish their research in peer-reviewed journals, acceptance for which is typically based on the quality of the study's statistical evidence. The relatively large amount of publicly available data about boards, however superficial, makes boards a prime topic for these researchers. What is troubling about this incentive scheme is that it encourages research that pinpoints a problem and proposes an appealing solution. Research of this type tends to paint an overly simplistic view of boards and, thus, proposes solutions that ignore the multifarious dynamics that affect board outcomes. This leads me to the third reason to study boards.

In theory, we study boards in order to gain insights that can help boards become more *effective* in real practice. As I have discussed in this essay, one of the greatest outcomes of *Pawns or Potentates* was its influence on how we think about and encourage positive action on corporate boards in practice. As in all of the sciences, informing practical application should be a central objective of any research project. It seems to me, however, that on this objective our current research paradigm falls short. When research fails to consider boards as the complex social systems that I deeply believe them to be, that research cannot have a real impact on the way boards function in real life. Researchers pursue topics about which they believe they will be able to find data without any true understanding of the impact of that data on the functioning of the board. If research continues down this road, we will fail to develop a modern understanding of how boards function *systemically*.

Let us return to the example of WorldCom. Investigations highlighted low levels of director participation as a direct cause of the company's collapse. How can a board be effective if some directors show up for only three to five hours a year? Clearly, the solution is to increase the number of hours that board members must spend doing board activities. Such one-stop solutions are common in the research literature today. However, although such a solution may be appealing in its promise of simplicity, it completely disregards the many other factors that influence boardroom behavior, including those that contribute to directors' disinterest in board activity in the first place. Unless researchers approach boards as dynamic social systems, they will continue to rely on reductive cause-and-effect explanations.

The review of this literature has left me with a concern that research about boards is being conducted primarily to help young scholars demonstrate their research skills. Given the methodologies that are being used and the failure to recognize the systemic properties of boards, much of the published research has not had positive ramifications for those who seek to improve board practice. My own belief is that this is not just a problem relevant to research about corporate boards, but that it in fact characterizes much of the research being conducted about organizations in general.

If one accepts Kuhn's idea of a paradigm — and I do — I think it is well time for scholars studying organizations to step back and reflect on the purposes of this academic research, especially that being published in peer-reviewed journals. Business institutions, not just boards, have flaws and problems. Certainly one purpose of academic research is to understand these issues, seek solutions, and hope to promote positive change. The study of boards is but one example where academics, young and old, are seeking to understand complex phenomena with mixed impact. The problem, as I have suggested earlier, is not the lack of effort or talents, but is, in my belief, the underlying concepts that guide organizational research. The basic fact is that these human institutions have systemic properties and cannot be studied through any other framework.

Too often, as we have seen in much of the research I have described, lip service is given to the fact that the institutions are systemic, while the actual gathering and conceptualization of data ignores that fact. It is important to not only recognize that boards and other organizational entities function as systems, but also to go forward with research methods and data that are aligned with that premise.

As I have noted, one of the barriers to understanding the systemic nature of boards is access to the actual behavior in the boardroom. It is important to recognize that there is no easy solution to this barrier when collecting data. My recommendation to young scholars, or to anyone else trying to capture the systemic properties of boards, is to use the methods that seem to have been most successful thus far: conducting surveys of directors about their experience. This method allows researchers to capture systemic properties of specific boards or boards as institutions more generally through the eyes of the directors who participate in boardroom activities themselves. Interviews are another plausible option, but they may be less useful given the logistical difficulties of arranging meetings with directors and the time constraints of the researcher. The important point to recognize: The barrier to attending board meetings does not prevent the researcher from getting a more robust picture of what happens in those meetings.

This paper reflects my own opinion and my frustration at the field's seeming movement away from the qualitative field work that is necessary in this type of research. However, I cannot deny the value of statistical analysis and I do recognize that the solution may require a combination of both quantitative and qualitative work. Through discussions with Westphal and Zajac, I can see a way in which the two methods may actually complement each other.[66] One option would be for researchers to develop hypotheses about board behavior based on real life observations or interviews with smaller groups of directors, and then to test those hypotheses against a larger dataset. Another method would begin with observing patterns in a dataset and then using field work to add color to those observations. Either way, there is room for both approaches in research on boards. How to collect the data to do both these types of research is still not obvious and remains the barrier to a complementary approach. What is most critical is that researchers and those who evaluate their work approach boards as systems and focus on the challenges that directors face *today*, so that findings may be both practical and relevant outside of academic journals.

---

[66]Conversation with James Westphal and Edward Zajac, September 21, 2016.

Appendices

A

Appendix

Exhibit 1

Zajac, Edward and John R. Kimberly, 'The Dynamics of CEO/Board Relationships,' in *The Executive Effect: Concepts and Methods for Studying Top Managers*, ed. D. Hambrick (Greenwich, CT: JAI Press, 1988) 179–204.	Research in governance and its relationship both to leadership and corporate strategy is relatively sparse. In this paper we argue that the nature of the relationships between the CEO and the board is both a significant gap and a particularity fertile domain for research on corporate performance. First we present summaries of four widely-reported corporate transitions, identifying common themes and generating a set of research questions. Next we suggest two theoretical perspectives which might help order the phenomena. Finally, we sketch out an agenda for researchers interested in these issues.
Westphal, James D. and Edward Zajac, 'Who Shall Govern? CEO/Board Power, Demographic Similarity, and New Director Selection,' *Administrative Science Quarterly* 40(1) (1995): 60–83.	This study examines CEO influence in the board of director selection process and the theoretical mechanism by which CEO influence is presumed to affect subsequent board decision making on CEO compensation. We address both of these issues by linking political and social psychological perspectives on organizational governance. We propose that powerful CEOs seek to appoint new board members who are demographically similar, and therefore more sympathetic, to them. Using a longitudinal research

	design and data on 413 Fortune/Forbes 500 companies from 1986 to 1991, we examine whether increased demographic similarity affects board decision making with respect to CEO compensation contracts. The results show that (1) when incumbent CEOs are more powerful than their boards of directors, new directors are likely to be demographically similar to the firm's CEO; (2) when boards are more powerful than their CEOs, new directors resemble the existing board; and (3) greater demographic similarity between the CEO and the board is likely to result in more generous CEO compensation contracts. We discuss the implications of the strong effect of demographic similarity for corporate control issues.
Zajac, Edward and James D. Westphal, 'Who Shall Succeed? How CEO/Board Preferences and Power Affect the Choice of New CEOs,' *Academy of Management Journal* 39(1) (1996): 64–90.	This study shows how social psychological and sociopolitical factors can create divergence in the preferences of an incumbent CEO and existing board regarding the desired characteristics of a new CEO, and how relative CEO/board power can predict whose preferences are realized. Using extensive longitudinal data, we found that more powerful boards are more likely to change CEO characteristics in the direction of their own demographic profile. Outside successors are also typically demographically different from their CEO predecessors but demographically similar to the boards.
Westphal, James D. and Edward Zajac, 'Director Reputation, CEO-Board Power, and the Dynamics of Board Interlocks,' *Administrative Science Quarterly* 41(3) (1996): 507–529.	This study advances research on CEO-board relationships, interlocking directorates, and director reputation by examining how contests for intraorganizational power can affect interorganizational ties. We propose that powerful top managers seek to maintain their control by selecting and retaining board members with experience on other, passive boards and excluding individuals with experience on more active boards. We also propose that powerful boards similarly seek to maintain their control by favoring directors with a reputation for more actively monitoring management and avoiding directors with experience on passive boards. Hypotheses are tested longitudinally using CEO-board data taken from 491 of the largest U.S. corporations over a recent

	seven-year period. The findings suggest that variation in CEO-board power relationships across organizations has contributed to a segmentation of the corporate director network. We discuss how our perspective can reconcile contrary views and debates on whether increased board control has diffused across large U.S. corporations.
Westphal, James D. and Edward Zajac, 'Defections from the Inner Circle: Social Exchange, Reciprocity, and the Diffusion of Board Independence in U.S. Corporations,' *Administrative Science Quarterly* 42(1) (1997): 161–183.	This study seeks to reconcile traditional sociological views of the corporate board as an instrument of elite cohesion with recent evidence of greater board activism and control over top management. We propose that CEO-directors may typically support fellow CEOs by impeding increased board control over management but that CEO-directors may also foster this change if they have experienced it in their own corporation. Drawing on social exchange theory, we develop and test the argument that these CEO-directors may experience a reversal in the basis for generalized social exchange with other top managers from one of deference and support to one of independence and control. Using data from a large sample of major U.S. corporations over a recent ten-year period, we show (1) how CEO-directors "defect" from the network of mutually supportive corporate leaders; (2) how defections have diffused across organizations and over time; and (3) how this has contributed to increased board control, as measured by changes in board structure, diversification strategy, and contingent compensation. We also provide evidence that a social exchange perspective can explain the diffusion of these changes better than more conventional perspectives on network diffusion that emphasize imitation or learning.
Golden, Brian R. and Edward Zajac, 'When Will Boards Influence Strategy?' *Strategic Management Journal* 22(12) (2001): 1087–1111.	While boards of directors are usually recognized as having the potential to affect strategic change in organizations, there is considerable debate as to whether such potential is typically realized. We seek to reconcile the debate on whether boards are typically passive vs. active players in the strategy realm by developing a model that specifies when boards are likely to influence organizational strategy and whether such an influence is likely to impel vs. impede change. Specifically, we develop arguments as

	to when certain demographic and processual features of boards imply a greater inclination for strategic change, when these features imply a greater preference for the status quo, and how differences in such inclinations will influence strategic change. We then also propose that a board's inclination for strategic change interacts with a board's power to affect change, generating a multiplicative effect on strategic change. These ideas are tested using survey and archival data from a national sample of over 3,000 hospitals. The supportive findings suggest that strategic change is significantly affected by board demography and board processes, and that these governance effects manifest themselves most strongly in situations where boards are more powerful. We discuss these findings in terms of their relevance for theories of demography, agency, and power.
Westphal, J.D. and M. Bednar, 'Pluralistic Ignorance in Corporate Boards and Firms' Strategic Persistence in Response to Low Firm Performance,' *Administrative Science Quarterly* 50 (2005): 262–298.	This study examines how a social psychological bias referred to as pluralistic ignorance may occur in corporate boards and how this bias could contribute to strategic persistence in response to relatively low firm performance. Our theory suggests that under conditions of low performance, there may be a systematic tendency for outside directors to underestimate the extent to which fellow directors share their concerns about the viability of the firm's corporate strategy. This reduces the propensity for individual directors to express their concerns about the current corporate strategy in board meetings, decreasing the likelihood that boards will initiate strategic change in response to low firm performance. We also posit factors that may moderate the extent to which pluralistic ignorance occurs on boards. We suggest that demographic homogeneity among outside directors (with respect to gender, functional background, education, and industry of employment) and the density of friendship ties among them will significantly moderate the occurrence of pluralistic ignorance on boards. We test our hypotheses with original survey data from a large sample of outside directors at medium-sized U.S. companies and find support for our theory. We discuss contributions of our theory and findings to the literatures on corporate governance, strategic persistence and change, and group decision-making processes in organizations.

Westphal, J.D. and I. Stern, 'Flattery Will Get You Everywhere (Especially If You Are A Male Caucasian): How Ingratiation, Boardroom Behavior, And Demographic Minority Status Affect Additional Board Appointments at U.S. Companies,' *Academy of Management Journal*, 50 (2007): 267–288.	This study examined influences on the likelihood that directors of U.S. corporations will receive additional board appointments. We tested hypotheses with original survey data from 760 outside directors at large and medium-sized U.S. firms. Supplementary analyses assessed post-Enron era generalizability. Directors increased their chances of board appointments via provision of advice and information to CEOs and ingratiatory behavior toward peer directors. Ethnic minorities and women were rewarded less on the director labor market for such behaviors. Directors also increased their appointment chances by engaging in low levels of monitoring and control behavior, and demographic minorities were punished more for such behaviors.
Stern, I., and J. D. Westphal, 'Stealthy Footsteps to the Boardroom: Executives' Backgrounds, Sophisticated Interpersonal Influence Behavior, and Board Appointments,' *Administrative Science Quarterly* 55 (2010): 278–319.	Drawing from theory and research on interpersonal attraction, as well as interviews with 42 directors of large U.S. industrial and service firms, we identified a set of social influence tactics that are less likely to be interpreted by the influence target as manipulative or political in intent and are therefore more likely to engender social influence. We consider who among top managers and directors of large firms is most likely to exercise such tactics and how their use affects the likelihood of garnering board appointments at other firms. An analysis of survey data on interpersonal influence behavior from a large sample of managers and chief executive officers (CEOs) at Forbes 500 companies strongly supports our theoretical arguments: managers' and directors' ingratiatory behavior toward colleagues is more likely to yield board appointments at other firms to the extent that it comprises relatively subtle forms of flattery and opinion conformity, which our theory suggests are less likely to elicit cynical attributions of motive. Supplementary analyses also indicate that these relationships are mediated by an increased likelihood of receiving a colleague's recommendation for the appointment. Moreover, we theorize and find that managers and directors, who have a background in politics, law or sales, or have an upper-class background, are more sophisticated and successful in their ingratiatory behavior.

Exhibit 2

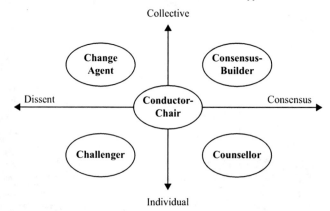

The Five Functional and Five Dysfunctional Director Behavioural Types

The Five Functional Director Behavioural Types*

*All functional directors rank high on the "persuasiveness" scale.

Source: Leblanc, Richard, and James M. Gillies, *Inside the Boardroom: How Boards Really Work and the Coming Revolution in Corporate Governance* (Mississauga, Ont: J. Wiley & Sons Canada, 2005), p. 166.

Exhibit 3

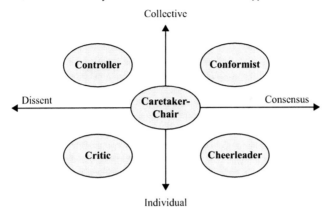

The Five Dysfunctional Director Behavioural Types*

*All dysfunctional directors rank low on the "persuasiveness" scale.

Source: Leblanc, Richard, and James M. Gillies, *Inside the Boardroom: How Boards Really Work and the Coming Revolution in Corporate Governance* (Mississauga, Ont: J. Wiley & Sons Canada, 2005), p. 167.

CPSIA information can be obtained
at www.ICGtesting.com
Printed in the USA
FFOW01n0820140317
33442FF